Parsippany-Troy Hills Library
Main Library
449 Halsey RD
Parsippany NJ 07054
973-887-5150

ANCIENT CHINESE TECHNOLOGY

JENNIFER CULP

ROSEN
PUBLISHING®

New York

Published in 2017 by The Rosen Publishing Group, Inc.
29 East 21st Street, New York, NY 10010

First Edition

Library of Congress Cataloging-in-Publication Data

Names: Culp, Jennifer, 1985– author.
Title: Ancient Chinese technology / Jennifer Culp.
Description: First edition. | New York : Rosen Publishing, 2017. |
 Series: Spotlight on the rise and fall of ancient civilizations |
 Audience: Grades 7–12. | Includes bibliographical references and index.
Identifiers: ISBN 9781477788998 (library bound) | ISBN
 9781477788974 (pbk.) | ISBN 9781477788981 (6-pack)
Subjects: LCSH: Technology—China—History—Juvenile literature. |
 Science—China—History—Juvenile literature. |
 Inventions--China—History—Juvenile literature. | Discoveries in
 science--History--Juvenile literature. | Civilization, Ancient—Juvenile
 literature.
Classification: LCC T27.C5 C835 2017 | DDC 609.31—dc23
LC record available at http://lccn.loc.gov/2016004443

Manufactured in the United States of America

CONTENTS

China is home to an ancient civilization responsible for what would later be termed "the Four Great Inventions": the magnetic compass, gunpowder, papermaking, and moveable type printing. These innovations influenced the course of the entire world. Chinese people also created the mechanical clock, the umbrella, the crossbow, fireworks, and porcelain pottery.

China measures its history in periods called dynasties named for the family who ruled during that time. Some dynasties were short, while others spanned hundreds of years. China's history reaches back far before the start of the Common Era when our current period of Western history began. (The year 2015, for example, is actually 2015 Common Era or 2015 CE.) The year 500 BCE occurred five hundred years before the start of the Common Era. China's story of invention and technological innovation goes back thousands and thousands of years before the beginning of the Common Era and modern history.

China is a cradle of civilization, home to billions of people and site in which some of the world's earliest known cultures developed.

By the time of the Shang dynasty (circa 1550–1050 BCE), the Chinese were quite advanced at metalworking. By this point they understood the properties of different metals and could apply this knowledge to create metal mixtures called alloys. The Chinese also developed a multipart mold system to make casts, or models, of metal objects. Bronze was the metal used to create vase-like ritual vessels to honor revered ancestors, although silver and gold were available. Unusually, practical metal implements such as farming tools were not created by the Chinese during this early period but were used instead for ritual purposes and worship. Early metal items were very exclusive and reserved for wealthy people. These ancient ritual vessels represent what one scholar termed "possibly the most remarkable achievement in the whole history of metalcraft before modern times."

Artifacts such as this Shang dynasty bronze ritual vessel demonstrate ancient Chinese artisans' skill with metal casting. This vase dates to the 12th century BCE.

O f all aspects of the Neolithic cultures in eastern China," states the Metropolitan Museum of Art's Department of Asian Art, "the use of jade made the most lasting contribution to Chinese civilization." Ancient Chinese people developed processes for carving jade—a beautiful, durable mineral also known as nephrite—as early as 3500 BCE. The colored stone was used for ceremonial as well as practical day-to-day purposes. Carved jade ritual objects, such as decorative weapons, have been found buried in the tombs of wealthy and powerful ancient Chinese people, where they are preserved and look just like new today. Such tools and weapons were treasured, and no wonder: jade is too hard to be carved with a knife and must be shaped through a difficult sanding process requiring incredible patience and skill. These jade weapons and statues reflect the values of the people with whom they lie buried.

This laboriously carved jade ax and its elaborate bronze handle were created during the Shang dynasty approximately 3000 years ago.

Porcelain is a type of ceramic, or clay, baked in an oven called a kiln at extremely high temperatures. It is smooth and white and has a shiny, shell-like texture. It is a very popular material for making dishes and, due to its place of origin, is also known as "china."

Early proto-porcelain ceramic work can be traced back to the Shang dynasty, approximately 1600 years BCE. These examples are not as advanced as later porcelain pieces, featuring yellow or brown hues and uneven thickness. Around the start of the Common Era, however, porcelain had been refined into the smooth white material we know today. Porcelain was not exported to Europe until thousands of years later during the Ming dynasty circa 1400 CE and was not produced in western Europe until three thousand years later during the 1700s. Although it looks delicate, porcelain is quite durable, and many examples of ancient Chinese porcelain works survive today.

China had long mastered the craft of fine porcelain ceramic by the mid-seventeenth century, when this flawless white vessel was created.

Archaeological exploration has revealed that the Neolithic Chinese peoples were sophisticated architects as well as builders. Foundations of buildings and structures were laid using a technique known as *hangtu*, or "rammed earth," in which layers of dirt were pounded together in order to create a secure base. Sections of the Great Wall of China that were built between 1000 BCE and the start of the Common Era depended on this type of rammed earth construction for stability. Since as far back as seven thousand years ago, Chinese buildings have relied on wooden framework for structural support. Joined wooden beams supported the building's roof, and the walls that separated individual rooms did not bear the weight of the whole structure. This technique, known as *dougong*, was developed and implemented widely between 770 and 475 BCE. This type of framework-supported wooden construction proved to be exceptionally resistant to earthquake damage.

Rammed earth construction allowed the Great Wall to expand through areas where stone was scarce and transportation of building material difficult.

The development of wooden plank roads has allowed Chinese people to travel safely along the steep sides of cliffs over the Yangtze River for thousands of years. The construction of these seemingly dangerous board walkways dates back to approximately between 475 and 220 BCE. Even though they were far from easy to navigate, the plank roads allowed for transportation at times when it would otherwise have been inconvenient or outright impossible, such as when the river flooded. In some cases, the plank roads were constructed using a technique that involved drilling holes into the side of the cliff, then stakes were inserted in order to support the planks. Other roads were chiseled, or carved, directly into the steep stone of the mountainsides. Also known as the Shu Roads, the plank pathways were described by Tang dynasty poet Li Bai as "ladders to heaven."

Just imagine climbing out along a steep cliff over a river to build a plank road in times before modern construction and safety equipment had been invented!

S ilk was first invented in China more than six thousand years ago. Silk is produced by a type of caterpillar called a silkworm that lives on a diet of mulberry leaves that grow in China. According to myth, the Chinese empress Leizu discovered the secret when a cocoon fell into her tea and unraveled, revealing a shining thread. However, as the silk-making process truly developed, it was sophisticated long before other peoples of the world dreamed of anything like the luxurious fabric; the oldest surviving piece of silk today dates back to 3630 BCE! Silk trading was a major driving force of communication and connection between China and other nations. For millennia, China was the world's sole producer of the shiny cloth, and demand throughout the world was so great that the extensive set of trade routes connecting China to southern and western countries came to be known collectively as the Silk Road.

This fourth- or fifth-century BCE Chinese silk survives on the ancient saddle blanket it decorates.

Like mulberry trees, tea plants are native to East Asia, and like silk, ancient China was famed for its export of tea. Legend credits the beverage's invention to the emperor Shennong around 2700 BCE, when some tea leaves accidentally blew into his drink of hot water. In reality, no one is sure precisely when the practice of drinking tea first developed. By the time of the Tang dynasty in 600 CE, tea as we know it today had become a popular drink worldwide. During this period, a writer named Lu Yu wrote a book titled *Ch'a Ching*, or *The Classic of Tea*, the earliest known essay on the caffeinated drink. Much of our current knowledge of tea's mysterious history comes from Lu Yu's writing, which detailed the drink's mythological origins and known history along with recipes for different flavors. However tea was originally invented, it certainly proved popular worldwide.

The lid on this Tang dynasty tea cup helped preserve the beverage's temperature, and also prevented debris from falling into the drink!

Ancient Chinese people began creating and consuming alcoholic beverages long before the start of recorded history. Remnants of Neolithic pottery found in the Stone Age–era village of Jiahu in northern China indicate that the people who lived there nine thousand years ago drank a fermented brew made from rice, honey, grapes, and hawthorn fruits. According to archaeochemist (one who applies scientific techniques to archaeology) Patrick McGovern, who performed chemical analysis to determine the contents of the ancient pottery, the fruity drink was most likely ingested at solemn occasions like funerals or religious ceremonies. According to McGovern, the ancient Jiahu residents' drink of choice defies modern classification. "It wasn't a beer, it wasn't a mead, and it wasn't a wine or a cider. It was somewhere between all of them, in this gray area," he said. "We called it a mixed beverage, because we're not sure where it fits in."

This Neolithic glass may have held the beverage that, in 2006, an American brewing company attempted to recreate.

Horses played a major role in the history of China, allowing for rapid transportation and effective military maneuvering. Horses were domesticated in China more than five thousand years ago and were clearly prized. The elite of the Shang dynasty around 1600 to 1100 BCE were even buried with horses and chariots. In later centuries, horses became vitally important to the practice of warfare. Around the fourth century BCE, China fell under threat from nomadic horse-riding tribes from the north and west. China's military held off invaders with mounted crossbowmen and increasingly fast and strong horses imported from neighboring lands. Advanced technology aided the Chinese military's defense effort: the Chinese people invented a harnessing system that helped control the horse while allowing it to breathe freely and also invented the stirrup to provide stability for the rider. Ceramic sculptures of horses dating from the Tang dynasty demonstrate the animals' importance to China's ruling class.

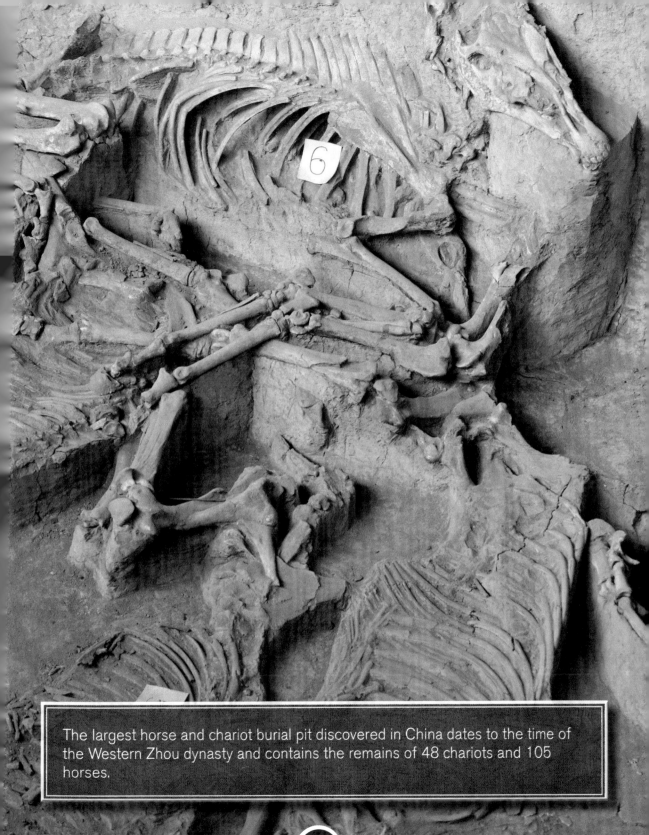

The largest horse and chariot burial pit discovered in China dates to the time of the Western Zhou dynasty and contains the remains of 48 chariots and 105 horses.

H orse-drawn chariots were used for transportation in China starting as early as 1400 BCE, five hundred years before horseback riding became popular. Like horseback riding, the chariot wasn't actually invented in China but spread in from surrounding countries. Chinese people made use of chariot technology for both transportation and warfare, however. War chariots were fitted with spoked bronze wheels and carried spearsmen, archers, and soldiers with axes into battle. States within China were ranked in order of power based on how many hundreds of war chariots they possessed. As the Chinese became more skilled at horseback riding and began to rely on cavalry—horseback-mounted soldiers—for military maneuvers, chariots fell out of use in fighting. Instead they were used for traveling long distances during times of peace. Members of Chinese royalty were often buried with chariots, with the belief that they could continue to travel in the afterlife.

The contents of China's largest known horse and chariot burial pit were entombed along with a ruler who was particularly noted for his military campaigns.

E vidence of the crossbow dates back to the sixth century BCE. The crossbow revolutionized the practice of warfare. Bow-and-arrow projectile weapons had existed for centuries but required a great deal of skill, strength, and expertise to operate effectively. The crossbow, which held a drawn bowstring in readiness to release a bolt at high velocity at the simple pull of a trigger, allowed any soldier to operate a powerful projectile weapon with little training. Crossbows were fully included into Chinese military operations by the Warring States period (about 475–221 BCE). Repeating crossbows, which could be reloaded and fired at a much faster rate, were also developed in the fourth century BCE. These weapons could probably fire as many as ten bolts in as few as fifteen seconds. There is little doubt that the invention of the crossbow contributed to China's long-lasting military dominance throughout Asia.

This bronze crossbow trigger mechanism from about 350 BCE features decorations of inlaid gold, suggesting that it probably came from a ceremonial weapon rather than a crossbow that saw hard use.

Few inventions would rock the world like the discovery of gunpowder. Chinese alchemist Wei Boyang is the first person known to have written about the chemical composition of gunpowder during the Han dynasty in 142 CE. He noted that a mixture of chemicals he combined would "fly and dance wildly." Approximately 150 years later in 300 CE, Chin dynasty scientist Ge Hong recorded a recipe for gunpowder. Gunpowder was not used in warfare until 900 CE. By 904 CE the Chinese military would use the explosive mixture to shoot rocks at high speeds out of hollow bamboo tubes, injuring and killing opponents. By 1044, an early form of bomb called a hand grenade was implemented, using the explosion of gunpowder to propel deadly shrapnel into opposing forces. By 1277, the Chinese military had developed land mines to use against invading Mongols. The oldest Chinese handgun ever discovered was made of bronze and dates from the year 1288.

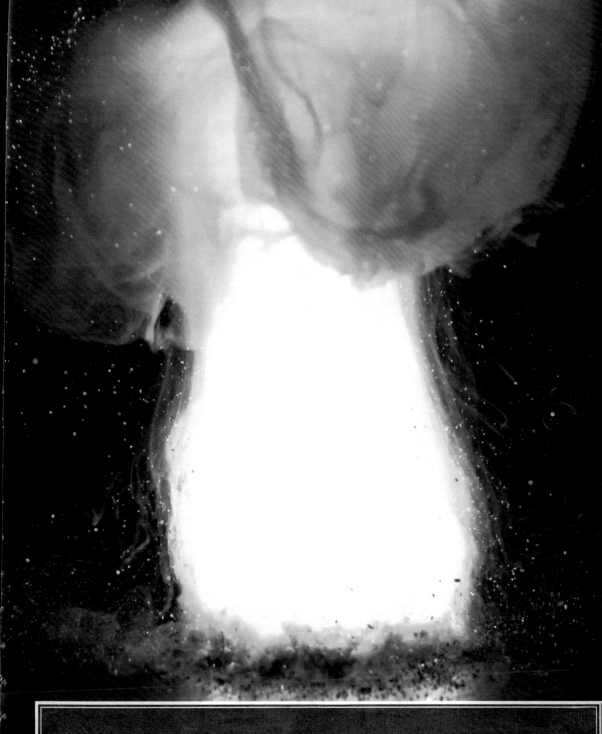

"Fly and dance wildly," indeed! A gunpowder explosion is bright, beautiful, and can propel metal shrapnel at deadly speeds.

Fireworks were a more beautiful and less (intentionally) deadly use of gunpowder that were first mentioned in texts dating from the seventh century CE. Originally the loud noises and bright lights created by pyrotechnic explosions were intended to frighten away evil spirits, but eventually they came to be commonly associated with celebratory gatherings. Rulers of the Tang dynasty were recognized for mounting stunning fireworks displays around 700 CE. Fireworks are strongly associated with celebration of the Chinese New Year, where their presence is intended to ward off evil spirits who may wickedly influence the luck in the approaching year for those who were celebrating. However, fireworks were also used violently in warfare to frighten the animals of the enemy as well as the combatants. They were even used to injure. Civilian pyrotechnicians continually improved upon explosive weapon designs to create fantastic aerial firework displays for peaceful enjoyment.

Fireworks are still a major part of New Year's Day celebrations in the People's Republic of China today.

The invention of paper is often credited to a Han dynasty court official named Cai Lun, who created a sheet of paper using mulberry fibers and other assorted materials around 105 CE. Paper was used for purposes other than writing in China for centuries previously, however, and surviving paper bearing Chinese writing from as far back as 8 BCE has been discovered. In addition to using paper for padding and wrapping goods such as tea and for writing, the Chinese pioneered the use of toilet paper for sanitary, or health, purposes! The rulers of the Song dynasty (about 960–1279 CE) issued printed paper money into circulation before any other government in the world, and Chinese people also used paper for entertainment in the form of playing cards. Papermaking technology slowly spread west over the trade routes of the Silk Road, where it reached western Europe by the tenth century CE.

Paper money proved more convenient for transport and transfer than other forms of currency, such as coins. This bill dates from the Yuan dynasty in 1287.

After paper was invented, writing became more convenient. Making multiple copies of books was still a problem, however, because it takes a long time to write out an entire book by hand. Around the year 1045 CE, a Chinese commoner named Bi Sheng changed the future of the entire world when he invented a system of moveable type printing. Bi Sheng made small ceramic pieces for each character of the Chinese language and their variants. When he wanted to print a text, he could rearrange the pieces in any order and print all the copies he wanted so he could make a copy of any book written. In the following centuries, Chinese scholars refined his system of moveable type by making wooden and then bronze printing pieces, but the basic technology remained the same. Chinese moveable type printing predated the European printing press by four hundred years and changed the whole world's access to literature and written information.

Bi Sheng's system of moveable type printing was still time-consuming, but it was much faster and more convenient than copying out entire manuscripts by hand with pen and ink.

THE VERY FIRST FOLDING UMBRELLAS

The world owes the Chinese credit for a now seemingly common item that revolutionized protection from bad weather: the folding umbrella. Historians believe the umbrella owes its origin to banners and flags of rank that preceded Chinese royalty during travel: the bigger the umbrella, the more important the person beneath it. When one particular emperor traveled, reports state, it took twenty-four servants just to carry his umbrella. Collapsible folding umbrellas were invented during the time of the Cao Wei dynasty between 200 and 300 CE. Umbrellas were originally made of silk and later from paper treated with wax or other material to make it waterproof. The bamboo or mulberry tree handle and frame of the umbrella were also treated in order to prevent mold or insect damage. Appropriately, the Chinese character for "parasol" resembles the shape of the object it describes, like a tiny drawing of an umbrella.

The umbrella offered weather protection from rain and sun and became popular worldwide, as pictured in Japan circa 1890.

MAGNETIC LODESTONE, AN EARLY COMPASS

S ince ancient times, the Chinese people were aware of the magnetic properties of lodestone, which was a naturally magnetized piece of the mineral known as magnetite. The world's first functioning compass was invented in China by the second century BCE. These compasses were made of a lodestone spoon resting on a smooth circular plate, which would rotate itself to rest on a north-south axis. As geophysicist Ronald T. Merrill, a scientist who studies the earth's physics, explains, "The discovery of the magnetic compass was an event of immense importance in science." The invention of the compass allowed for accurate navigation even when the sun was obscured. Originally, however, it was used to orient houses in accordance with the principles of feng shui and to search for likely locations of rare gems. The compass did not become available for use in western Europe until the twelfth century CE.

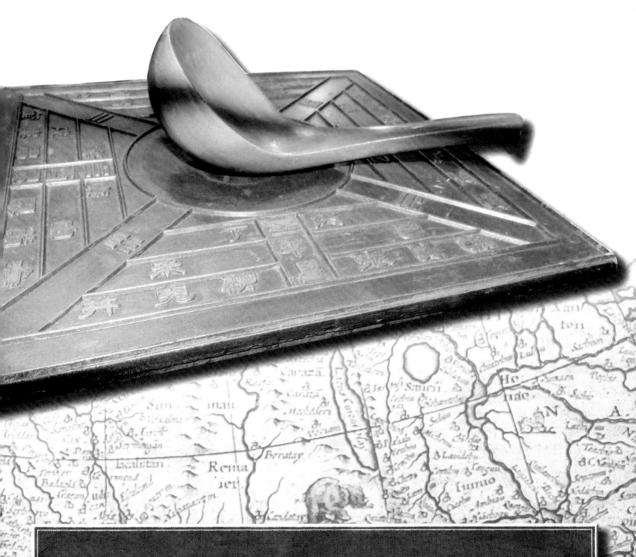

The handle of an ancient Chinese lodestone compass always points south, just as the needle of the compasses we use today points toward the north.

MECHANISM OF THE MECHANICAL CLOCK

Yi Xing, a Buddhist monk who studied astronomy, mathematics, and engineering, along with Tang government official and engineer Liang Lingzan, constructed the world's first mechanical clock mechanism around 725 CE. Yi Xing and Liang Lingzan's clock didn't look much like a modern clock, but it successfully implemented escapement, the process that keeps the clock moving at a regular pace so that it can keep time. Su Song, a famed Chinese scientist of the Song dynasty, built upon the work of Yi Xing and Liang Lingzan to create a massive astronomical clock tower in 1088 CE. Su Song's clock relied on the weight of moving water to keep the clockwork mechanism turning at regular intervals. Like so many other lasting ancient Chinese technological advancements, Su Song's clock tower was so innovative that it influenced the development of clockwork mechanisms in China for centuries afterward. It eventually lead to the creation of clocks powered by falling sand instead of water.

Su Song's water-balance escapement mechanism turned the hands of the clock regularly as falling water turned the escapement wheel.

GLOSSARY

aerial In the air, as opposed to on the ground.

alloy A man-made mixture of two or more metals.

cast A model of an object formed by pouring molten metal into a mold and allowing it to harden.

ceramic Hardened clay that has been baked in a high-temperature oven called a kiln.

dougong A building technique in which a wooden framework supports the weight of the roof, and walls are built independently to separate rooms.

dynasty A ruling family line of China; Chinese history is divided into periods called dynasties named for the family that ruled during that time period.

escapement The process by which a clock uses the energy of a moving mechanism to turn and keep time regularly.

feng shui A system in which buildings and structures are organized in a fashion believed to maximize harmony with surrounding natural forces.

ferment The process by which yeasts and bacteria convert carbohydrates in a liquid into alcohol.

hangtu A building technique in which layers of earth were pounded together to make a solid base to support walls and buildings.

mead An alcoholic drink made by fermenting honey and water.

millennium A period of one thousand years.

Neolithic The Neolithic period refers to the later part of the Stone Age, when a culture had developed stone weapons and tools.

pyrotechnics The science of combining chemicals to make a self-contained explosion—a firework.

shrapnel Small pieces of metal, stone, or wood projected violently by an explosion.

FOR MORE INFORMATION

Asian Art Museum
200 Larkin Street
San Francisco, CA 94102
(415) 581-3500
Website: http://www.asianart.org
This museum displays art from from prehistory to the present.

Asia Society Museum
725 Park Avenue
New York, NY 10021
(212) 288-6400
Website: http://asiasociety.org/arts/asia-society-museum
This organization promotes understanding and partnership between
    Asia and the United States in art, business, culture, and policy.

Calgary Chinese Cultural Center
197 First Street SW
Calgary, AB T2P 4M4
Canada
(403) 262-5071
Website: http://www.culturalcentre.ca
The center fosters cultural exchange and promotes multiculturalism.

WEBSITES

Because of the changing nature of Internet links, Rosen Publishing has
developed an online list of websites related to the subject of this book.
This site is updated regularly. Please use this link to access the list:

http://www.rosenlinks.com/SRFAC/ctech

FOR FURTHER READING

Branscombe, Allison. *All About China: Stories, Songs, Crafts, and More for Kids*. North Clarendon, VA: Tuttle Publishing, 2014.

Forbes, Scott. *Not for Parents China: Everything You Ever Wanted to Know*. Oakland, CA: Lonely Planet, 2012.

Harper, Damian. *Lonely Planet China*. Oakland, CA: Lonely Planet, 2015.

He, Li, and Michael Knight. *Power and Glory: Court Arts of China's Ming Dynasty*. San Francisco, CA: Asian Art Museum, 2016.

Huo, Christina. *Chinese New Year Picture Book: Spring Festival Facts and Stories for Kids and Adults*. New York, NY: Amazon Digital Services, Inc., 2015.

Jian, Li. *Ming's Adventure with Confucius in Qufu: A Story in English and Chinese*. Shanghai, China: Shanghai Press, 2015.

Keay, John. *China: A History*. New York, NY: Basic Books, 2011.

Lin, Jillian. *The Emperor Who Built the Great Wall (Once Upon a Time in China)*. Charleston, SC: CreateSpace Independent Publishing Platform, 2015.

Nunes, Shiho. *Chinese Fables: The Dragon Slayer and Other Timeless Tales of Wisdom*. North Clarendon, VA: Tuttle Publishing, 2013.

O'Connor, Jane. *Hidden Army: Clay Soldiers of Ancient China* (All Aboard Reading). New York, NY: Grosset & Dunlap, 2011.

Qicheng, Wang. *The Big Book of China*. New York, NY: Amazon Digital Services, Inc., 2015.

Roche, Jess. *Jaw-Dropping Geography: Fun Learning Facts About the Great Wall of China*. Charleston, SC: CreateSpace Independent Publishing Platform, 2015.

Tse, Brian. *Bowls of Happiness: Treasures from China and the Forbidden City*. New York, NY: China Institute in America, 2015.

Yen Mah, Adeline. *China: Land of Dragons and Emperors*. New York, NY: Ember, 2011.

BIBLIOGRAPHY

Cohen, Jennie. "Fireworks Vibrant History." History in the Headlines, July 1, 2011 (http://www.history.com/news/fireworks-vibrant-history).

Department of Asian Art. "Neolithic Period in China." Heilbrunn Timeline of Art History. The Metropolitan Museum of Art. October 2004 (http://www.metmuseum.org/toah/hd/cneo/hd_cneo.htm).

Ebrey, Patricia, and Anne Waltham. *East Asia: A Cultural, Social, and Political History*. Wadsworth, MA: Cengage Learning, 2006.

Jian, Xiao. "Lu Yu and Chinese Tea Culture." China.com: Gourmet. July 10, 2004 (http://english.china.com/zh_cn/gourmet/tea/11020889/20040710/11776099.htm).

Jump, David. "An Introduction to the 'Hard Roads to Shu,' their Environment, History, and Adventures Since Ancient Times." 2010, revised April 2015 (http://www.qinshuroads.org/docs/html/Shu_Roads_Introduction.htm#_ftn2).

Kelun, Chen. *Chinese Porcelain: Art, Elegance and Appreciation*. San Francisco, CA: Long River Press, 2004.

Kentucky Horse Park: International Museum of the Horse. "The Horse in Chinese History: A Brief Overview." Kentucky Educational Television, 2016. Retrieved December 2015 (https://www.ket.org/artofthehorse/ed/history.htm).

Linduff, Katheryn, and Jianjun Mei. "Metallurgy in Ancient Eastern Asia: How Is It Studied? Where Is the Field Headed?" Presented to the Society for American Archaeology Annual Meeting in Vancouver. The British Museum, 2008 (http://www.britishmuseum.org/pdf/Linduff%20Mei%20China.pdf).

Lu Yu. *The Classic of Tea*. Francis Ross Carpenter, trans. Boston, MA; Little, Brown and Company, 1974.

Mark, Joshua J. "Silk Road." Ancient History Encyclopedia, March 28, 2014 (http://www.ancient.eu/Silk_Road).

Merrill, Ronald T., and Michael W. McElhinny. *The Earth's Magnetic Field: Its History, Origin and Planetary Perspective.* New York, NY: Academic Press Inc. Ltd., 1983.

Mikkolainen, Terhi. "Chinese Inventions: Umbrellas and Parasols." GB Times, May 18, 2007 (http://gbtimes.com/life/chinese-inventions-umbrellas-and-parasols).

Payne-Gallwey, Ralph. *The Crossbow.* Longman's, Green & Co., 1903 (http://www.atarn.org/chinese/rept_xbow.htm).

Ramey, David, and Paul Buell. "A True History of Acupuncture." *Focus on Alternative and Complementary Therapies*, Vol. 9, issue 4, December 2004.

Roach, John. "9,000-Year-Old Beer Re-Created from Chinese Recipe." National Geographic News, July 18, 2005 (http://news.nationalgeographic.com/news/2005/07/0718_050718_ancientbeer.html).

Rounds, Alex. *Leizu: Empress of the Silkworm.* LearningIsland.com, 2006.

Soda, Craig. *The Dangerous, Disastrous, Unusual History of War.* North Mankato, MN: Capstone Press, 2012.

Steinhardt, Nancy Shatzman. *Chinese Imperial City Planning.* Honolulu, HI: University of Hawaii Press, 1990.

Steinhardt, Nancy Shatzman. "Mapping the Chinese City: The Image and the Reality." From *Envisioning the City: Six Studies in Urban Cartography*, David Buisseret, ed. Chicago, IL: University of Chicago Press, 1998.

Vainker, Shelagh. *Chinese Silk: A Cultural History.* New Brunswick, NJ: Rutgers University Press, 2004.

Xinian, Fu, et al. Nancy Steinhardt, ed. *Chinese Architecture.* New Haven, CT: Yale University and New World Press, 2002.

Yang, Lihui, and Deming An. *Handbook of Chinese Mythology.* New York, NY: Oxford University Press, 2005.

Yangtze Yan, ed. "New Evidence Suggests Longer Paper Making History in China." Chinaview.cn News, August 8, 2006 (http://news.xinhuanet.com/english/2006-08/08/content_4937457.htm).

INDEX

ABOUT THE AUTHOR

Jennifer Culp is a medical editor and author of nonfiction books for children and young adults, most recently, *The Totally Gross History of China*.

PHOTO CREDITS